Today's Sports Stars

Puka Nacua
Football Star

by Charlie Beattie

www.focusreaders.com

Copyright © 2026 by Focus Readers®, Mendota Heights, MN 55120. All rights reserved. No part of this book may be reproduced or utilized in any form or by any means without written permission from the publisher.

Focus Readers is distributed by North Star Editions:
sales@northstareditions.com | 888-417-0195

Produced for Focus Readers by Red Line Editorial.

Photographs ©: Paul Spinelli/AP Images, cover, 1; Kevin Terrell/AP Images, 4, 25; Michael Conroy/AP Images, 6, 29; Shutterstock Images, 8; Christopher Mast/Icon Sportswire, 11; Tyler Ingham/Icon Sportswire, 12; Steph Chambers/Getty Images Sport/Getty Images, 14; Thearon W. Henderson/Getty Images Sport/Getty Images, 16; Ryan Kang/Getty Images Sport/Getty Images, 19; Nic Antaya/Getty Images Sport/Getty Images, 20; Katelyn Mulcahy/Getty Images Sport/Getty Images, 23; Red Line Editorial, 27

Library of Congress Cataloging-in-Publication Data
Library of Congress Cataloging-in-Publication Data is available on the Library of Congress website.

ISBN
979-8-88998-595-2 (hardcover)
979-8-88998-621-8 (paperback)
979-8-88998-612-6 (ebook pdf)
979-8-88998-604-1 (hosted ebook)

Printed in the United States of America
Mankato, MN
082025

About the Author

Charlie Beattie is a writer, editor, and former sportscaster. Originally from Saint Paul, Minnesota, he now lives in Charleston, South Carolina, with his wife and son.

Table of Contents

CHAPTER 1

Overtime Winner 5

CHAPTER 2

Football Fanatic 9

CHAPTER 3

Star Rookie 15

CHAPTER 4

Making History 21

At-a-Glance Map • 26

Focus Questions • 28

Glossary • 30

To Learn More • 31

Index • 32

CHAPTER 1

Overtime Winner

Los Angeles Rams receiver Puka Nacua sprinted to the 10-yard line. The score was tied in **overtime**. Nacua turned around. Quarterback Matthew Stafford fired a pass. Nacua leaped and caught it.

Puka Nacua catches a pass in overtime during a 2023 game against the Indianapolis Colts.

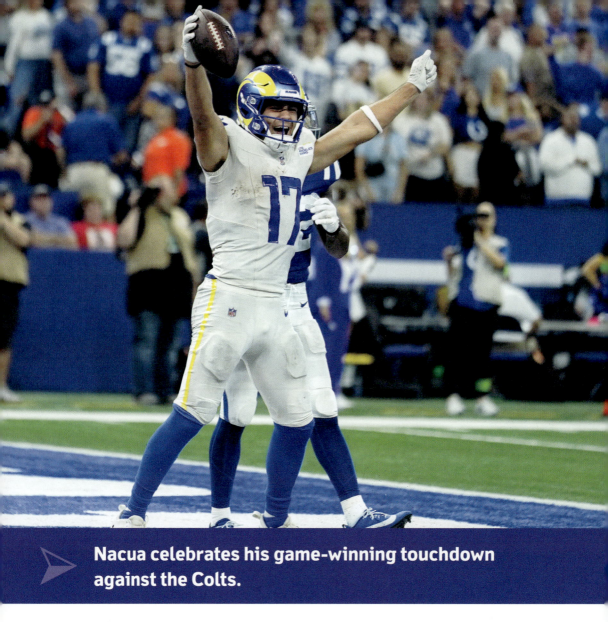

Nacua celebrates his game-winning touchdown against the Colts.

The **rookie** landed and turned. Two defenders stood in front of Nacua. He **juked** past one. The second defender tried to wrap Nacua up. But Nacua broke free. Then he dived into the end zone. The Rams had won! Nacua picked a perfect time to score his first touchdown in the National Football League (NFL).

Did You Know?
Nacua didn't know he'd beaten the Colts until his teammates told him. During the NFL regular season, a touchdown in overtime wins the game.

CHAPTER 2

Football Fanatic

Makea "Puka" Nacua was born in Las Vegas, Nevada, on May 29, 2001. Puka's father, Lionel, died when Puka was 11 years old. The loss was very hard for Puka. He relied on his family for support.

 In 2001, more than 500,000 people lived in Las Vegas, Nevada.

Puka's mother, Penina, moved the family to Provo, Utah.

Puka has four brothers and one sister. He grew up playing football with his brothers Samson and Kai. They helped one another become stars. In high school, Puka led his team to a state championship.

Did You Know?

Nacua's real name is Makea. *Puka* means "chubby" in Samoan. Nacua was a chubby baby and got the nickname then.

Puka Nacua makes a play during a 2019 game with the Washington Huskies.

Many colleges recruited Puka. He spent his first two years at the University of Washington. But he wanted to be closer to his family.

Nacua makes a game-winning touchdown catch in a 2022 game with BYU.

So, he switched to Brigham Young University (BYU) in Utah.

Nacua became a star at BYU. His quarterbacks knew they could trust him. Nacua always seemed to make the tough catches. In two seasons, Nacua had 11 touchdown catches. But he also got hurt a lot. That made NFL teams worry about his future.

Before the 2023 NFL **Draft**, Nacua ran the 40-yard dash for **scouts**. He didn't run as fast as he'd hoped. Many teams decided not to draft him. But the Los Angeles Rams took a chance. They selected Nacua with the 177th pick. He was off to the NFL.

CHAPTER 3

Star Rookie

Many players picked low in the draft don't play much. But in 2023, Puka Nacua played right away. In Week 1, the Rams needed a big play. Nacua caught a pass from quarterback Matthew Stafford.

Puka Nacua had 119 receiving yards in his first NFL game.

Nacua set a rookie record with 1,486 receiving yards.

Nacua spun away from a tackle. He sprinted to the 1-yard line. The Rams scored on the next play.

The next week, Nacua racked up 15 catches. No rookie had ever caught more passes in a game.

Nacua kept setting records. For example, he finished the year with 105 catches. That was the most ever for a rookie.

Nacua showed the league his many talents. For instance, he was tough and ready to block for others.

Did You Know?
Before games, Nacua practices visualization. He imagines playing well that day. He closes his eyes and watches himself perform.

Nacua was also smart on the field. He could read a defense and respond quickly. That helped him get wide open.

    The Rams made the **playoffs** in the 2023 season. They faced the Detroit Lions. In the second quarter, Nacua bolted down the sideline. Stafford threw a bomb downfield. Nacua caught it and sprinted for the end zone. Then he juked past two defenders. He scored a 50-yard touchdown. However, the

In his first playoff game, Nacua piled up 181 receiving yards. That set a rookie playoff record.

Rams ended up losing 24–23. It was a tough end to an amazing rookie season.

CHAPTER 4

Making History

In 2024, Puka Nacua hoped for a great start to his second season. But he hurt his knee early in the first game. He missed the next five games.

Puka Nacua runs with the ball during Week 1 of the 2024 season.

The Rams won only two games with Nacua out. When he came back, he provided a big boost. In Week 8, he caught seven passes for 106 yards. Los Angeles won 30–20 over the Minnesota Vikings.

Going into Week 14, the Rams had improved to 6–6. Then they had a big game against the Buffalo Bills. The Rams led 38–35 late in the game. Nacua caught a pass. He sprinted past defenders for a touchdown. The Rams won 44–42.

Nacua leaps into the end zone for a touchdown during a 2024 game against the Buffalo Bills.

Nacua finished the game with more than 160 receiving yards. He also scored a rushing touchdown and a receiving touchdown. No Rams player had ever done all those things in one game.

The Rams made the playoffs again. And this time, they had a home game. Then disaster struck. Wildfires spread through Los Angeles. To stay safe, Nacua had to **evacuate**. He stayed with a teammate.

Did You Know?
For some games, Puka Nacua wears shoes supporting the **Diabetes Foundation**. Nacua's father died from diabetes.

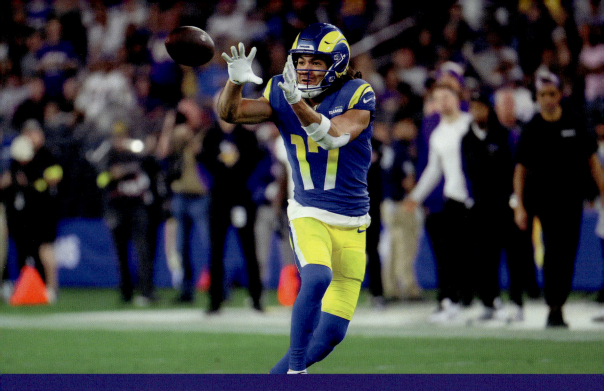

Nacua had 322 playoff receiving yards in his first two seasons in the NFL.

The playoff game was moved to Arizona. Even so, the Rams crushed the Vikings 27–9. The next week, the Rams got knocked out of the playoffs. But fans couldn't wait to see what Nacua would do next.

AT-A-GLANCE MAP

Puka Nacua

- Height: 6 feet, 2 inches (188 cm)
- Weight: 212 pounds (96 kg)
- Birth date: May 29, 2001
- Birthplace: Las Vegas, Nevada
- High school: Orem High School (Orem, Utah)
- College: University of Washington (Seattle, Washington) (2019–20); Brigham Young University (Provo, Utah) (2021–22)
- NFL team: Los Angeles Rams (2023–)
- Major awards: Second Team All-Pro (2023); Pro Bowl (2023); All-Rookie Team (2023)

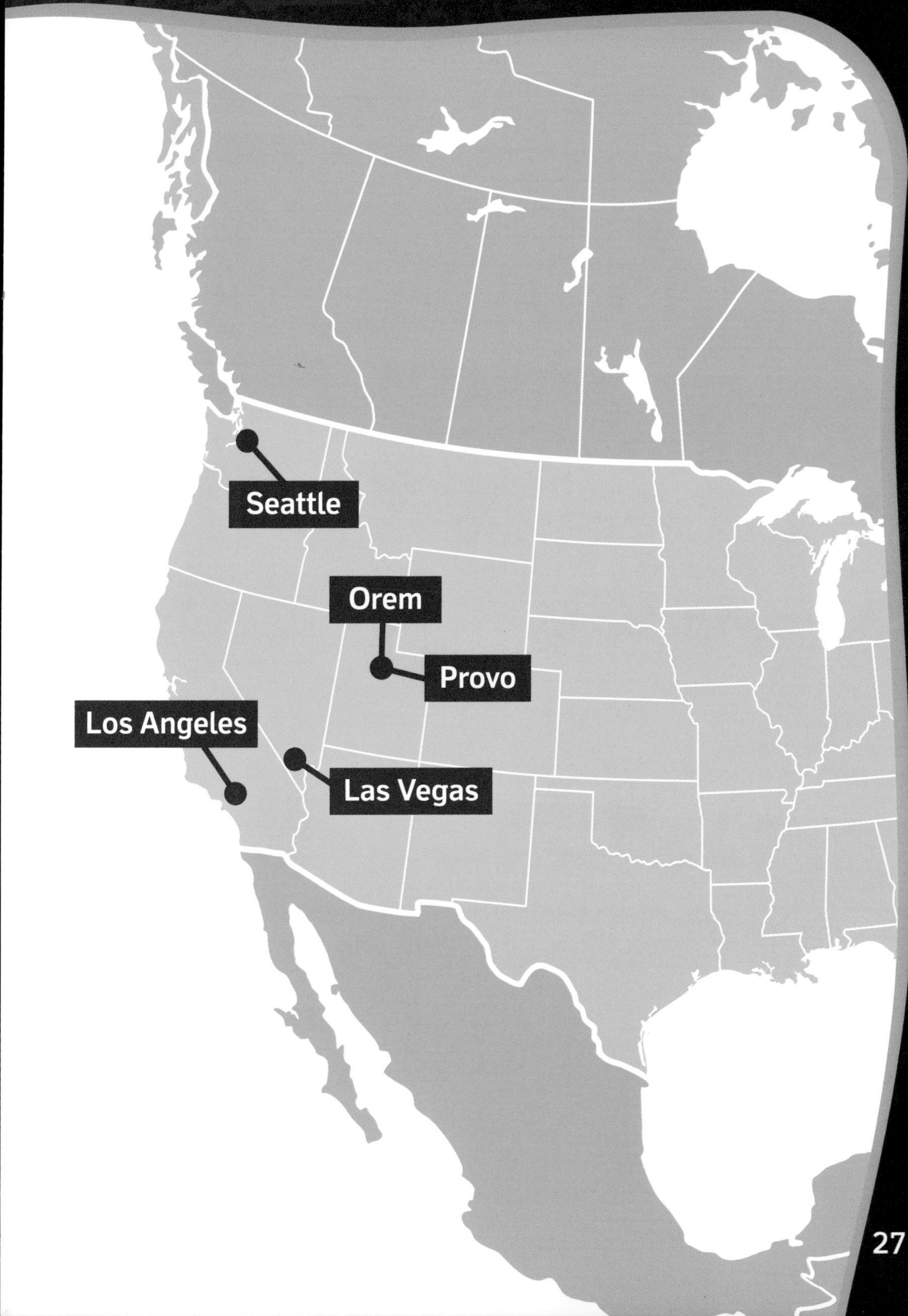
Seattle
Orem
Provo
Los Angeles
Las Vegas

Focus Questions

Write your answers on a separate piece of paper.

1. Write a paragraph that explains the main ideas of Chapter 3.

2. Would you like to play wide receiver? Why or why not?

3. Why did Puka Nacua leave Washington and go to BYU?
   - A. He wanted to play quarterback.
   - B. He wanted to be closer to his family.
   - C. He wanted to make more money.

4. Why was Nacua taken so late in the NFL Draft?
   - A. Teams thought he wasn't fast enough.
   - B. Teams thought he was too short.
   - C. Teams thought he wanted to play professional baseball.

5. What does **recruited** mean in this book?

*Many colleges **recruited** Puka. He spent his first two years at the University of Washington.*

    A. ignored someone
    B. turned someone down
    C. invited someone to join

6. What does the term **visualization** mean in this book?

*Before games, Nacua practices **visualization**. He imagines playing well that day. He closes his eyes and watches himself perform.*

    A. imagining a result to help make it happen
    B. studying people's past mistakes
    C. playing well during a game

Answer key on page 32.

Glossary

diabetes
A disease that affects how the body breaks down energy and blood sugar.

draft
A system that allows teams to acquire new players coming into a league.

evacuate
To leave a place of danger.

juked
Faked out an opponent.

overtime
An extra period to determine a winner in a tie game.

playoffs
A set of games played after the regular season to decide which team will be the champion.

rookie
A professional athlete in his or her first year.

scouts
People whose jobs involve looking for talented young players.

To Learn More

BOOKS

Coleman, Ted. *Los Angeles Rams All-Time Greats*. Press Box Books, 2022.

Flynn, Brendan. *Los Angeles Rams*. Apex Editions, 2025.

Scheffer, Janie. *The Los Angeles Rams*. Bellwether Media, 2024.

NOTE TO EDUCATORS

Visit **www.focusreaders.com** to find lesson plans, activities, links, and other resources related to this title.

Index

B
Brigham Young University, 12
Buffalo Bills, 22

D
Detroit Lions, 18
Diabetes Foundation, 24
draft, 13, 15

H
high school, 10

L
Las Vegas, Nevada, 9

M
Minnesota Vikings, 22, 25

N
Nacua, Lionel, 9
Nacua, Penina, 10

P
playoffs, 18, 24–25
Provo, Utah, 10

S
scouts, 13
Stafford, Matthew, 5, 15, 18

V
visualization, 17

W
Washington, University of, 11
wildfires, 24

Answer Key: 1. Answers will vary; 2. Answers will vary; 3. B; 4. A; 5. C; 6. A